haiku: the mood of earth

VENETIA VALLEY K-8
177 N SAN PEDRO ROAD
SAN RAFAEL, CA 94903

he mood of earth/ Ann Atwood

Charles Scribner's Sons *New York*

To Joan

who knows the place is Here

and the time is Now

This book published simultaneously in the
United States of America and in Canada.
Copyright under the Berne Convention

A—8.71[PZ]

Printed in the United States of America
by Princeton Polychrome Press, Princeton, N.J.
Designed by Bernard Klein
Library of Congress Catalog Card Number 70-162737

haiku: the mood of earth

No verse form is as closely related to art as the three-line oriental haiku. Haiku has been called the poetry of sensation, but primarily, it is a visual experience. An understanding of haiku, however limited it must be in this brief introduction, should yield a deeper insight into the principles applied in art and photography. All art springs from the same fountain, and many of the techniques used in writing good haiku can also be used in making good pictures.

The haiku form itself, bound within the limitations of approximately seventeen syllables, is paradoxical in nature. It is both simple and profound, constrictive and expansive, meticulously descriptive and yet wholly suggestive. And it is the very limitations of haiku that demand the discipline necessary to all art. For with this meagre allowance of words, the poet must not be tempted to stop at the right word, but must enlarge his search until the *only* word is within his grasp.

Nor must the artist or photographer stop short of this same "only"—the one object, the one angle, the one possible slant of light which alone can express the fullness of his experience.

By linking itself with nature, with the moods of earth and the cycles of the seasons, the haiku telescopes in a single word a limitless range of sensations and ideas which are part of man's common fund of experience. One noun can swing the reader into spaceless flight.

So each of the season's names excite endless associations accompanied by emotional overtones. The mind spins outward on a far journey at the sound of these words: autumn, spring, winter, summer. For man, being made of earth, is sensitive to its every mood. Dusk . . . rain . . . forest . . . grass . . . these are more than nouns. They are the essence of being.

The pattern of the haiku itself suggests the rhythm

of breathing. Its length is the length of a breath drawn in, held for a moment of wonder, and then released. The written haiku is the re-creation of this moment of wonder, or this "haiku-moment," in which a purer quality of light illumines that which the eye sees, lifting it to new levels of interpretation. It was the radiance of such a moment which enabled William Blake to "see the world in a grain of sand."

Yet it is not solely his own experience which the true artist seeks to convey. The greater the art, the more clearly the viewer or the reader recognizes the artist within himself. This is the highest aim of haiku—to allow the reader the full spectrum of response. The poet induces this artistic impulse from the reader by harmonizing the three elements essential to every haiku: time, place, and object. The time is Now—yet in this Now is a sense of timelessness. The place is Here—yet in this Here is the hint of everywhere. And the object placed in its poetic setting generates intuitive waves of meaning in the mind of the reader.

For the word "haiku" literally means *beginning*. It is begun by the writer and completed by the reader. This creative balance is destroyed if the poem overflows with the poet's own feeling:

> *This gathering dark . . .*
> *alone with the last gull I feel*
> *an unknown sadness.*

The writer's role is more the role of a painter, presenting the scene in such a way as to evoke sadness in the reader:

> *This gathering dark . . .*
> *a sharp wave driving skyward*
> *the last hungry gull.*

Here both writer and reader, each in his own way,

can experience the poetic power of the moment. Since this direct contact with nature is achieved by specific haiku techniques, one wonders how far photography can explore this ancient art of painting with words. Are some of its elements, successful for so many centuries, adaptable to other art forms?

A haiku may be simply a vividly presented scene suffused with poetic feeling; yet often a single idea or detail is isolated and brought into close focus. This detail can create a second image totally unlike the first, yet rising naturally out of it:

> *Musing on a gnarled*
> *tree-root my mind leaps as a*
> *stallion rears up!*

This deeper look—this second glance—provides a method for expressing a haiku by using two pictures.

Another technique often used is to magnify one fragment of the whole, letting it ripple in the reader's mind into wider and wider overtones:

> *In a sea creature's shell*
> *flashing in waves of sunlight*
> *—the waking of wings!*

It is by this two-picture method—this concentration of attention from the long view to the close-up—that this book suggests the haiku-moment might also be pursued by a camera. In the pages that follow it might be said that the words illustrate the photographs, the three lines being divided in such a way as to unite the two pictures into one haiku.

This book is asking: can art and photography, by applying some of the haiku principles, find an effective way of getting inside nature and seeing it from the heart out? And is it possible to thrust off into that spaceless haiku flight without the wings of words?

A blank page of sand—

at the water's cutting edge

the pattern shaping.

In a sea creature's shell

flashing in waves of sunlight

—the waking of wings!

Half mocking the sea

the gulls dip within reach of

each exploding wave.

Ebb tide at sundown . . .

Now clouds of foam no longer

blur the bright mirror.

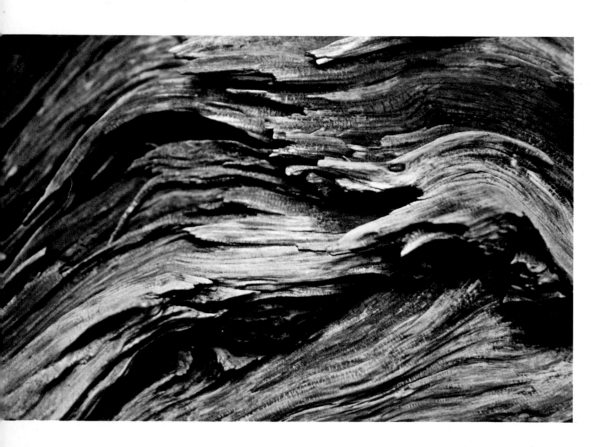

On wood returning

from a long sea journey

the deeper print of waves.

Musing on a gnarled

tree root

my mind leaps

as a stallion rears up!

The curved lines

of the distant pond—

      how sharp and straight

at the water's edge.

The swift growth of spring.

Colt mothered in the meadow

now you are alone.

SUN VALLEY SCHOOL
75 HAPPY LANE
SAN RAFAEL, CALIFORNIA 94901

Clouds of heaven and

trees of earth

　　　　merge into one

in the still river.

Sea rocks blown with fog . . .

Time locked in mist

long long forgotten.

The hand of a leaf

splitting and sifting the air.

—The blueness of breath!

Egrets on their way south—

The water left with

broken shadows

Trailing diamonds—

Green leaf dying . . .

What do they say, these inked letters

on yellow parchment?

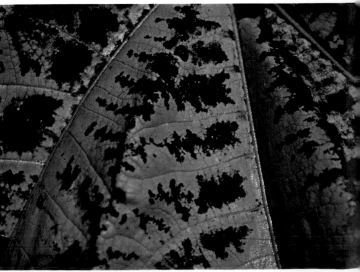

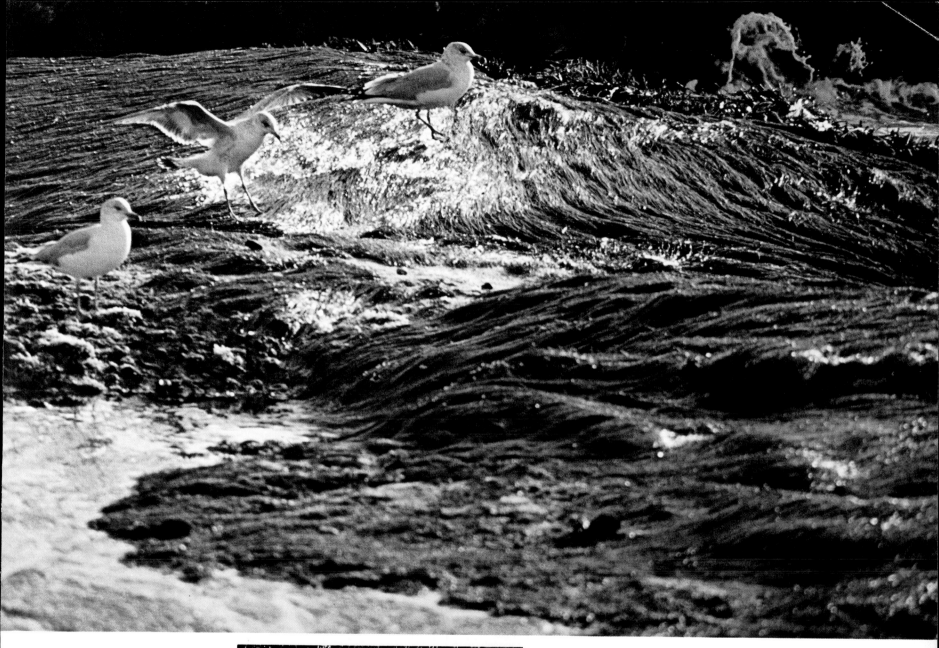

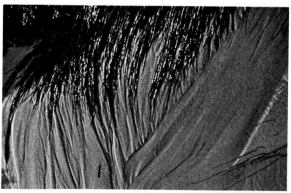

Cold lick of the sea . . .

The birds fleeing from it

the grass flowing with it.

Gull with the starry prints

do you stand here and watch

these ballets in the sand?

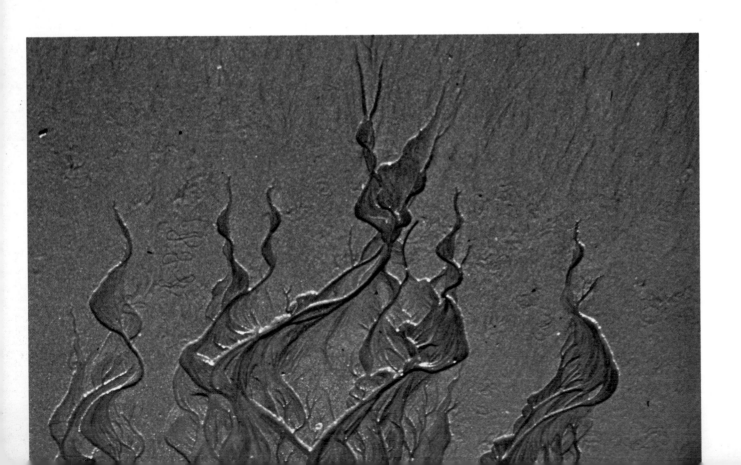

The cooing murmurs
of doves . . .

the blur of dreams

the scent of lost summers.

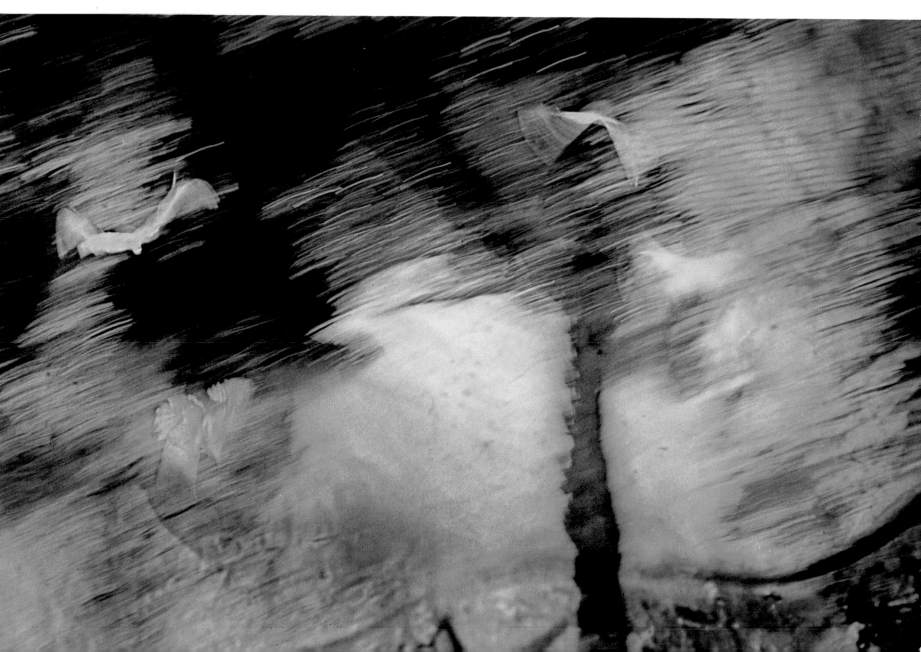

The brook leaps the steep

mountain

from every hollow

a swirl of new joy!

In the pool's shadowy

pocket lies autumn's plunder

of copper and gold.

Part of the growing

pattern now

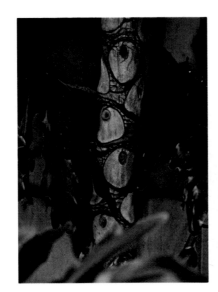

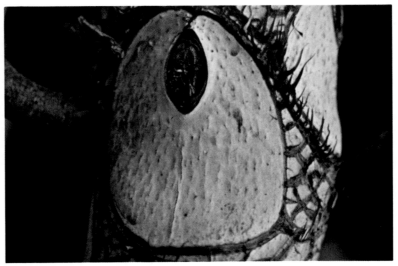

the tears of plants

no longer flowing.

Summer dying . . .

In drying grasses

one last sun

so slowly setting.

Summer in Eden

still hushed and hidden,

guarded

by the flaming sword.

Through dripping branches

the woods and I are one

in the eyes of the rain.

On the tree's bright trunk

at day's end . . . its leaf, its life

written in shadow.

The light of bright leaves . . .
Tonight a pinwheel spinning
on the rim of sleep.

This empty mountain!
The thinning trail you travel
is ravelled in mist.